# A Grandmother's Love

Published by: Latonya Hadley
Text Copyright: © by Latonya Hadley

Bible quotations are taken from The King James Study Bible. Copyright © 1988 by Liberty University, Thomas Publishers.

**ISBN: 978-0-578-62541-6**

# __Dedication__

This book is dedicated to A'Maria Tyler.
In memory of her grandmother, Carrie Nesbitt.

Honesty is a 5-year-old, bright minded, little girl from Florida. People like to call it the Sunshine State. She really loves her mommy and daddy. However, her grandmother had a special place in her heart, and it seemed as if she loved her grandmother more than her mommy and daddy.

"Hi, Mommy! Where is Grandma?" asked Honesty. She always asked for grandma. You see Honesty had a different type of love for her grandmother. She loved her grandmother with everything in her.

Grandma was the one who always bailed Honesty out of trouble. She was Honesty's protector and safe place as every grandparent should be.

Every Saturday morning, Honesty looked forward to going out around the town with Grandma.

Ring, Ring! "It's Grandma!" Honesty yelled with the sound of excitement coming from her voice.

"Yes, baby! It's Grandma! Would you like for me to pick you up?" Grandma asked.

"Yes, Yes! I'm going to get dressed now. Can we go to Playland Toy Store to buy some new toys?" asked Honesty. It wasn't just the shopping that Honesty liked. She loved Grandma and enjoyed spending time with her.

"Yes, baby! We can go to Playland Toy Store. Grandma doesn't have a lot of money, so I can only buy one toy," said Grandma.

Honesty appreciated the one toy and the ride to Playland Toy Store because it allowed her to spend time with the one person, she loved with all her heart.

But one day things turned for the worst. Grandma had a bad fall.

"What is wrong with Grandma?" Honesty asked her mom.

"Baby, Grandma had a bad fall and she's going to have to spend a few days in the hospital so the doctor can make her feel better," replied Honesty's mom.

Unfortunately, that was not the case. Grandma began to get sicker and sicker.

Honesty's spirits were still very high because every chance she was awarded, she went to the hospital with her mom just so she could spend time with Grandma.

While in the hospital Grandma would tell Honesty how much she loved her, and how special she was to her.

The sound of Grandma's voice really melted Honesty's heart because Grandma was her safe place.

Grandma's health began to decline. She did not look or sound the same. Honesty's mom decided not to allow Honesty to continue to go to the hospital to visit Grandma.

"Mommy, when will I be able to go to the hospital to see Grandma again?" Honesty asked.

Mommy didn't know how to respond to Honesty because she didn't want to hurt Honesty's heart.

"As soon as Grandma get a little better, we will go and see her," exclaimed Honesty's mom.

Honesty started to miss her Grandma more and more. She started to repeat the Bible scripture she learned in church about healing for her Grandma.

Isaiah 53:5 states, "He was wounded because of our rebellious deeds, crushed because of our sins; he endured punishment that made us well because of his wounds we have been healed."

On February 16, Honesty was out enjoying a day with her mom and dad when they received a telephone call from the doctor.

The doctor stated that Grandma's life had come to an end. Honesty's mom was devastated. The only thing she could think of was the hurt that it would cause Honesty. Mommy and Daddy discussed how they would break the terrifying news to Honesty. They wanted to be as gentle with her heart as possible.

"Baby! Let's have a talk," stated Honesty's mom as she touched the top of her head. A river of tears began to roll down Honesty's mom eyes as she began to tell the heartbreaking news to Honesty. The look of sorrow was all over Honesty's face.

"Honesty, God loves us all very much. We are not physically placed in this world forever, but our spirits are," proclaimed Honesty's mom.

"God allows us time to experience one another. God called Grandma home with him today because she has work in heaven to do with the angels. This means she will no longer be here on earth with us anymore," explained Honesty's mom.

Honesty immediately began to scream and cry. Even at the tender age of five, Honesty knew exactly what her Mommy's words meant.

"So, I'll never get to see Grandma again! Will God ever send her back?" asked Honesty as tears rolled down her eyes and the look of sadness covered her face.

"Unfortunately, no baby! You will not have the chance to see her on earth again, but you can always talk to her in the spirit. If you are going through anything, you can talk to her. If you want to say something to her…say it. I promise you she can hear it," stated Honesty's mom with comfort.

Honesty walked around for quite some time in sadness. Her mommy always reminded her that in her time of sadness to pray and ask God to comfort her so He can fill her sadness with joy.

Psalms 30:5 states, "Weeping may endure for a night, but joy comes in the morning." Honesty returned to school the next day. Her classmates greeted her with hugs, cards, and smiles. This made Honesty feel loved all over again! However, there were some students who didn't understand.

There were times that Honesty would get sad at home and at school because of the loss of her Grandma. Honesty didn't want to say goodbye to Grandma.

With all the love around her, she still felt afraid and alone because Grandma was gone. She was reminded of Psalms 56:3 that says, "When I am afraid, I put my trust in you."

Honesty began to lack focus in school. Her grades also began to drop. She was bullied by children who didn't understand what it felt like losing someone close to you. Those students didn't understand Honesty's pain and thought it was funny.

There were children that would laugh at her and say, "Ha, ha, ha! That's why your Grandma died."

Honesty was heartbroken by the cruel and insensitive hearts of some of the children at her school.

Ephesians 4:29 says, "When you talk, do not say harmful things. But say what people need—words that will help others become stronger. Then what you say will help those who listen to you."

Honesty did not know how to cope with the loss of someone so close to her heart; someone she loved dearly. Honesty's mom knew that this was a wound that even time couldn't heal. She knew that this was a wound that only God could heal.

Honesty's mom hurt came from losing a mother. However, it disappointed her more to watch Honesty cope with the pain and the loss of losing her best friend and grandmother.

The only thing she could do to comfort Honesty was hold her as tight as she could, pray for her, and let her know that she is loved. Honesty's mom reminded her that she is loved just as much as Grandma did and that God loves her even more.

Nehemiah 8 states, "Do not grieve, for the joy of the Lord is your strength." As time passed and the more Honesty and her mom began to pray, she started to receive joy again. Honesty learned that Grandma was now an Angel that was in a better place.

Honesty learned that Grandma would always love her whether she was near or far. Most importantly, she learned that God called Grandma home so that she may rest and do the work of God as one of his most precious Angels.

www.ingramcontent.com/pod-product-compliance
Lightning Source LLC
LaVergne TN
LVHW072102070426
835508LV00002B/227